Grammaropolis
PRESENTS

Student Workbook
GRADES 3-5

written by
THE MAYOR OF GRAMMAROPOLIS

HOUSTON

Edited by Christopher Knight
Cover and Interior Design by Mckee Frazior
Character Design by Powerhouse Animation & Mckee Frazior

ISBN: 9781644420201
Copyright © 2020 by Grammaropolis LLC
Illustrations copyright © 2020 by Grammaropolis LLC
All rights reserved.
Published by Six Foot Press
Printed in the U.S.A.

Grammaropolis.com
SixFootPress.com

Table of Contents

Table of Contents

FROM THE DESK OF THE MAYOR

There's a reason students can instantly recall everything that happened in their favorite movies but struggle to retain much of the important information you're trying to cover in school: people are hard-wired to remember what we connect with on an emotional level.

That's why grammar is so hard to teach. (As a former grammar teacher myself, I know firsthand.) Traditional materials are dry, abstract, and lifeless. There's nothing to connect with. Put simply, grammar is boring.

But it doesn't have to be! Our story-based approach combines traditional instruction with original narrative content, appealing to different learning styles and encouraging students to make a deeper connection with the elements of grammar.

In Grammaropolis, adverbs don't just modify verbs; adverbs are bossy! They tell the verbs **where** to go, **when** to leave, and **how** to get there. A pronoun doesn't just replace a noun; Roger the pronoun is a shady character who's always trying to trick Nelson the noun into giving up his spot.

And it works! Our mobile apps have already been downloaded over 2.5 million times, and thousands of schools and districts use our web-based site license. In other words, we don't skimp on the vegetables; we just make them taste good.

Thanks so much for visiting Grammaropolis. I hope you enjoy your stay!

— *The Mayor*

Meet the Punctuation Department!

Meet the End Marks

We're the end marks! We come at the end of a sentence.

We indicate whether a sentence is demonstrative, interrogative, or exclamatory.

EXAMPLES

DECLARATIVE: Learning grammar can be fun.

INTERROGATIVE: Learning grammar can be fun?

EXCLAMATORY: Learning grammar can be fun!

Meet Officer Period (a.k.a. Full Stop)

I'm a period.
In some parts of the world,
I'm called a full stop.

I make a sentence declarative.

I come at the end of a
statement, request, or
mild command.

EXAMPLES

STATEMENT: I know you enjoy eating chocolate.

REQUEST: Please share your chocolate with me.

MILD COMMAND: Don't eat my chocolate, though.

Grammaropolis

Using Periods (Full Stops)

Use me at the end of statement, a request, or a mild command.

Statement:
I could use your help with this.

Request:
Please help me with this.

Mild Command:
Help me with this.

Pro Tip:
A sentence ending in a period is called a **declarative** sentence.

Pro Tip:
Outside the United States, I'm called a Full Stop.

Let's practice!

Instructions:
Add periods to the following sentences if they are needed, then circle all of the periods that you've added.

EXAMPLE:
I am tired. I want to go home. Aren't you tired?

1. Please don't talk that way to my puppy

2. Henry likes cheese Henry likes pizza Why does Henry hate cheese pizza?

3. Andy and Darlene both tripped on the log

4. Serve yourself some beans Don't spill them, though

5. Cricket is an interesting sport I wasn't aware of that

Your turn!

Instructions:
Write declarative sentences to state information about the topics below. Remember to circle the periods when you use them.

1. cheese _____

2. clouds _____

3. soccer _____

Meet Detective Question Mark

Am I not a question mark?

Do I not make a sentence interrogative?

Do I not come at the end of a question or turn a statement into a question?

EXAMPLES

QUESTION: Do you know any famous musicians?

STATEMENT: My friend Kyle is a famous musician.

STATEMENT INTO QUESTION: Your friend Kyle is a famous musician?

Using Question Marks

Pro Tip:
A sentence ending in a question mark is called an **interrogative** sentence.

Let's practice!

Instructions:
Add question marks to the following sentences if they are needed, then circle all of the question marks that you've added.

EXAMPLE:

Why is that restaurant so expensive? Is it because the tables are real wood?

1. What is your name I bet your name is a family name.

2. Jimmy is yelling. What is he yelling about

3. When is the book fair Is it tomorrow, or is it today

4. Why are you here

5. Some people are funny. Some people aren't funny. Which kind of person are you

Your turn!

Instructions:
Write interrogative sentences (questions) to gather information about the topics below. Remember to circle the question marks when you use them.

1. sandwiches _____

2. trees _____

3. hairstyles _____

Meet Sergeant Exclamation Mark

I'm an exclamation mark!

I make a sentence exclamatory!

I come after an exclamation or a strong interjection!

EXAMPLES

EXCLAMATION: That chocolate cake is enormous!
I am so excited to eat that cake!

INTERJECTION: Hey! I haven't finished yet.
Uh oh! I ate way too much.

Using Exclamation Marks

Use me at the end of an exclamation or after a strong interjection.

Exclamation:
That's Nelson's platypus!

Strong Interjection:
Hey! That's Nelson's platypus.

Pro Tip:
A sentence ending in an exclamation mark is called an **exclamatory sentence**.

Let's practice!

Instructions:
Add exclamation marks to the following sentences if they are needed, then circle all of the exclamation marks that you've added.

EXAMPLE:
That restaurant is really expensive! Wow!

1. Of course That looks amazing

2. A coyote is chasing me Help

3. Give that to me right this minute

4. Look out There's a truck speeding toward us

5. Eureka I just thought of a brilliant idea

Your turn!

Instructions:
Write exclamatory sentences that incorporate the strong interjections below. Remember to circle the exclamation marks when you use them.

1. Ouch _____

2. Eek _____

3. Oh no _____

Writing with the End Marks

INSTRUCTIONS (PART ONE):
Write five declarative sentences, using periods as the end marks, and circle the periods.

1. _____

2. _____

3. _____

4. _____

5. _____

INSTRUCTIONS (PART TWO):
Turn those declarative sentences into interrogative sentences, using question marks as the end marks.
(It's not just a matter of adding a question mark!) Circle the question marks.

1. _____

2. _____

3. _____

4. _____

5. _____

INSTRUCTIONS (PART THREE):
Turn those sentences into exclamatory sentences, using exclamation marks as the end marks. Feel free to add interjections, and circle all the exclamation marks.

1. _____

2. _____

3. _____

4. _____

5. _____

The Big End Marks Quiz!

INSTRUCTIONS: Indicate which of the following sentences is **declarative.**

1. A. Have you ever been to the opera?
   B. I finally went to the opera last night.
   C. I love the opera!

2. A. My mother is shorter than my son.
   B. Can you believe that my mother is shorter than my son?
   C. Oh my! I can't believe that my mother is shorter than my son!

3. A. Hand me those cookies immediately!
   B. Hand me those cookies immediately.
   C. Did you grab those cookies when i wasn't looking?

INSTRUCTIONS: Indicate which of the following sentences is **interrogative.**

4. A. Do you have any idea who that person is?
   B. I have never met that person before in my life.
   C. Stop asking me about that person!

5. A. This bed is incredibly comfortable!
   B. I don't generally enjoy sleeping on beds that are too comfortable.
   C. Have you ever slept on the ground?

6. A. How many fingers am I holding up?
   B. Don't point your fingers at me like that.
   C. Things are looking up!

INSTRUCTIONS: Indicate which of the following sentences is **exclamatory.**

7. A. Just sit back, relax, and enjoy the drive.
   B. How much longer until we get there?
   C. I hate driving!

8. A. That's one way to think about it!
   B. What, exactly, are you thinking?
   C. I think it's time to put our pencils away.

9. A. Do you like movies about polar bears?
   B. Let's watch that movie about polar bears.
   C. You're always talking about polar bears!

Grammaropolis

Meet Chief Comma

I am a comma.

I may have a lot of rules, but my mission is simple.

I separate words and word groups for one reason: to keep your writing clear.

EXAMPLES

WITH ITEMS IN A SERIES: He ordered a burger, fries, and a drink.

WITH INDEPENDENT CLAUSES: My friend missed school, so I helped her with her homework.

WITH SUBORDINATE CLAUSES: After my friend missed school, she had a lot of work to do.

Using Commas in a Series

Use me to separate items in a series of three or more words or word groups.

With a Series of Words:
My sandwich is huge, messy, and delicious.

With a Series of Word Groups:
I found bugs in the sink, on the bookshelf, and under the table.

Pro Tip:
The **serial comma** (Oxford comma) is used before a coordinating conjunction in a series. Although it's technically not mandatory, we suggest always using the serial comma to avoid confusion.

Pro Tip:
Word groups can be phrases or clauses.

Let's practice!

Instructions:
Add commas to the following sentences if they are needed, then circle all of the commas that you've added.

EXAMPLE:

I like to read fantasy, science fiction, and historical fiction.

1. The birds were chirping the sun was shining but Jerome was still unhappy.

2. Please buy peas carrots potatoes celery and tomatoes for my stew.

3. Summer camp is where I practiced archery made bracelets and met new friends.

4. The apple in my lunch is big red and juicy.

5. I'm inviting Keisha Jasmine Ricky and Francisco to my party.

Your turn!

Instructions:
Write sentences containing lists of three or more words or word groups. Remember to use the serial comma, and don't forget to circle all the commas you use.

1. _____

2. _____

3. _____

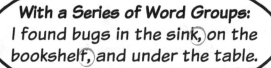

Using Commas with Independent Clauses

Use me before a coordinating conjunction when joining two or more independent clauses.

I like cheese, and I like bread.

I like cheese, but I don't like bread.

I like cheesy bread, so I will order some.

Pro Tip:
The FANBOYS are the coordinating conjunctions *for, and, nor, but, or, yet,* and *so.*

Let's practice!

Instructions:
Add commas to the following sentences if they are needed, then circle all of the commas that you've added.

EXAMPLE:
Those people are funny, but I don't know their names.

1. I was looking down so I didn't trip on the curb.

2. Justine was hungry and thirsty but there was nothing for her to eat or drink.

3. Devin did his homework but he forgot to turn it in.

4. Please help me look for my ring for I have lost it.

5. I am happy for my brother is here but I will be sad when he leaves.

Your turn!

Instructions:
Join another independent clause to each of the independent clauses below by using commas and coordinating conjunctions. Don't forget to circle the commas.

1. Sheila likes apple pie _____

2. I don't know Jason _____

3. Roslyn followed the rules _____

Using Commas with Subordinate Clauses

Use me after an introductory subordinate clause.

Subordinate Clause First:
After we ate dinner, we ran home.

Subordinate Clause Second:
We ran home *after we ate dinner.*

Pro Tip:
A *subordinating conjunction* introduces a subordinate (dependent) clause.

Pro Tip:
The subordinate clause can come before or after the independent clause. If it comes after, there is no comma between the clauses.

Let's practice!

Instructions:
Add commas to the following sentences if they are needed, then circle all of the commas that you've added.

EXAMPLE:

If you go to my house, you will probably meet my brother.

1. Don't blame me if the food is terrible.

2. Although school doesn't start for another hour some students are already here.

3. When you get to Spain you should definitely have paella for dinner.

4. Debbie will be in a better mood after she finishes her homework.

5. Unless you tell me otherwise I will assume that you aren't hungry.

Your turn!

Instructions:
Write complete sentences using each of the subordinating conjunctions below to introduce a subordinate clause. Don't forget to circle any commas you use!

1. unless _____

2. whenever _____

3. if _____

Writing with Commas

INSTRUCTIONS:
Use commas to write sentences that contain a series of words. Circle the commas.

1. _____

2. _____

3. _____

4. _____

INSTRUCTIONS:
Circle four of the FANBOYS (coordinating conjunctions) and then write sentences that use commas to join independent clauses with the FANBOYS you've chosen. Circle the commas!

> FANBOYS: for and nor but or yet so

1. _____

2. _____

3. _____

4. _____

INSTRUCTIONS:
Circle four subordinating conjunctions and then write sentences that incorporate subordinate and independent clauses. Remember that you only use a comma when the subordinate clause is introductory. Circle the commas!

> after although as because before if once since so though unless until whenever wherever while

1. _____

2. _____

3. _____

4. _____

Grammaropolis

The Big Comma Quiz!

INSTRUCTIONS: Indicate which of the following sentences uses correct comma punctuation.

1. A. I went to my room, so that I could get some sleep.
   B. I went to my room, so I missed the rest of the movie.
   C. I went to my room so I missed the rest of the movie.

2. A. Whenever Carla eats chocolate chips, she feels like a superhero.
   B. Carla feels like a superhero, whenever she eats chocolate chips.
   C. Whenever Carla eats chocolate chips she feels like a superhero.

3. A. My favorite foods are all on sale: apples, pears cheese, chocolate, and bread.
   B. My favorite foods are all on sale: apples, pears, cheese, chocolate, and bread.
   C. My favorite foods are all on sale: apples, pears, cheese chocolate, and bread.

4. A. Kevin is hungry, so he is going to the store for some food.
   B. Kevin is hungry, so, he is going to the store for some food.
   C. Kevin is hungry so, he is going to the store for some food.

5. A. Lionel ran out of cheese, chocolate, and bread because Kevin ate it all.
   B. Because Kevin ate it all Lionel ran out of cheese chocolate, and bread.
   C. Lionel ran out of cheese, chocolate, and bread, because Kevin ate it all.

6. A. You must let me go onstage for I am the greatest singer of my generation.
   B. You must let me go onstage, for I am the greatest singer of my generation.
   C. You must let me go onstage for, I am the greatest singer of my generation.

7. A. After we eat, we must wash the dishes, and we must be careful.
   B. After we eat, we must wash the dishes, and be careful.
   C. After we eat we must wash the dishes and be careful.

8. A. Dax tripped, he fell but he tried not to cry.
   B. Dax tripped and he fell but he tried not to cry.
   C. Dax tripped, and he fell, but he tried not to cry.

9. A. George offered to help, so I sent him to the store.
   B. George offered to help so I sent him to the store.
   C. George offered to help so, I sent him to the store.

10. A. My dog ate my backpack, my homework, my snack, and my shoe.
    B. My dog ate my backpack my homework my snack, and my shoe.
    C. I love my dog but I am really annoyed at how much he eats.

Meet Sheriff Semicolon

I am a semicolon.

I connect related independent clauses without the FANBOYS.

I also connect independent clauses after conjunctive adverbs and transitional expressions.

EXAMPLES

WITH INDEPENDENT CLAUSES: Kendra is coming over tomorrow; I need to clean my room.

AFTER CONJUNCTIVE ADVERBS: Kendra doesn't like playing in messy rooms; consequently, I should clean mine.

AFTER TRANSITIONAL EXPRESSIONS: I'm going to clean my room; as a result, it will be clean for Kendra's visit.

Grammaropolis

Using Semicolons to Connect Independent Clauses

> Use me to connect two related independent clauses without the FANBOYS.

> **Separate Sentences:**
> It is hot today. Jason is thirsty. I'm have a big presentation tomorrow. I am nervous.

Pro Tip:
Use a semicolon when you want to show a close connection between independent clauses.

> **One Sentence with a Semicolon:**
> It is hot today; Jason is thirsty. I have a big presentation tomorrow; I am nervous.

Let's practice!

Instructions:
Join the independent clauses below by adding semicolons wherever they are needed. Circle the semicolons.

EXAMPLE:

It snowed last night; I can't wait to go outside!

1. The members of the Donner party were starving they had run out of food.

2. Elmer finished his homework it was time to have some fun.

3. I was in a hurry at the grocery store I forgot to buy chocolate.

4. Stevie can't help you move that couch he hurt his back yesterday.

5. Neha is shining the flashlight in my eyes I can't see anything.

Your turn!

Instructions:
Write three sentences that use semicolons to join two independent clauses. Don't forget to circle the semicolons when you use them.

1. _____

2. _____

3. _____

Grammaropolis

Using Semicolons with Transitional Expressions

Use me to join two independent clauses with a transitional expression (a transitional phrase or a conjunctive adverb).

Transitional Phrase:
Kelli didn't get enough sleep last night; as a result, she is exhausted.

Conjunctive Adverb:
Kelli is exhausted; nevertheless, she got to school on time.

Pro Tip:
Common transitional phrases include: *after all, for example, as a result,* and *in conclusion.*

Pro Tip:
Common conjunctive adverbs include: *however, furthermore, nevertheless, also,* and *finally.*

Let's practice!

Instructions:
Add semicolons to the following sentences if they are needed, then underline the transitional expressions and circle the semicolons you've added.

EXAMPLE:
I am tired; <u>therefore</u>, I will go to bed soon.

1. That box looks heavy as a result, I need to be careful moving it.

2. Bethany read three books over the summer conversely, Fritz didn't read any books.

3. My dog is old nevertheless, she has a lot of energy.

4. Lucius doesn't eat cheddar cheese in fact, he doesn't eat cheese at all.

5. You owe me a favor therefore, you're going to wash the dishes tonight.

Your turn!

Instructions:
Use semicolons with the following transitional expressions to write sentences that join two independent clauses. Don't forget to circle the semicolons.

1. on the other hand _____

2. meanwhile _____

3. however _____

Writing with Semicolons

INSTRUCTIONS (PART ONE):
Write three simple sentences.

EXAMPLE: _____I think it's going to rain today._____

1. _____

2. _____

3. _____

INSTRUCTIONS (PART TWO):
Now use a semicolon to join a related independent clause to each of your sentences above. Circle the semicolon in each sentence.

EXAMPLE: _____It's going to rain today; I need to pack an umbrella._____

1. _____

2. _____

3. _____

INSTRUCTIONS (PART THREE):
Now, circle three of the following transitional expressions and use them with semicolons to add different independent clauses to your original sentences. Circle the semicolon in each sentence.

accordingly also meanwhile anyway moreover however consequently indeed therefore otherwise after all   in fact   as a result   for example   on the other hand   at any rate   even so   in conclusion

EXAMPLE: _____It's going to rain today; as a result, I bet they cancel soccer practice._____

1. _____

2. _____

3. _____

Grammaropolis

I am a *colon*.

I can introduce a list, quotation, or explanation that comes after an independent clause.

EXAMPLES

INTRODUCING A LIST: I have three items to buy at the store: potato chips, ice cream, and napkins.

INTRODUCING A QUOTATION: Lyall told me why she didn't do her homework: "I was too tired."

INTRODUCING AN EXPLANATION: The solution is clear: you must buy me a bigger birthday cake.

Using Colons to Introduce Lists

> Use me after an independent clause if you want to introduce a list.

> I always bring three drinks on a picnic: water, soda, and lemonade.
>
> Suki invited four people to her birthday party: George, Alan, Vicky, and Sandra.

> Remember to use your commas correctly!

Pro Tip:
Make sure that the clause that comes before the colon is an independent clause.

Let's practice!

Instructions:
Add colons to the following sentences if they are needed, then circle all of the colons that you've added.

EXAMPLE:

The kids talked about the usual things: homework, friends, and electronics.

1. I bought all the necessary ingredients butter, flour, sugar, and milk.

2. We visited lots of countries last year Italy, Denmark, Mexico, and Chile.

3. You have lots of chores making your bed, washing the dishes, and pulling weeds.

4. Sandra enjoys many hobbies knitting, surfing, and disco dancing.

5. Annie has many favorite animals lions, hedgehogs, koalas, and marmots.

Your turn!

Instructions:
Use colons after independent clauses to introduce lists about the topics below. Don't forget to circle the colons.

1. foods _____

2. family members_____

3. clothes _____

Using Colons with Quotations and Clarifications

Use me after an independent clause to introduce a quotation or to clarify or emphasize.

Quotation:
Jaime told his mom about his day: "I had a great time at school!"

Clarification:
The solution is clear: you must give me a cookie.

Emphasis:
I came here for one thing: chocolate.

Pro Tip:
If you're going to use a colon like this, be sure that it follows an independent clause.

Let's practice!

Instructions:
Add colons to the following sentences if they are needed, then circle all of the periods that you've added.

EXAMPLE:
Jessie talked about his favorite toys: "I love things that don't have batteries."

1. There's something you have to know I don't like watching television.

2. At least we agree on something strawberries are tasty.

3. Sandra gave a strange explanation for her behavior "I was asleep the whole time."

4. There was only one way Xavier wanted to spend his weekend asleep.

5. Jason spent the whole day complaining about the same thing "My feet hurt."

Your turn!

Instructions:
Write sentences that use a colon after an independent clause to introduce a quotation, to clarify, and to provide emphasis. Don't forget to circle the colons.

1. Quotation _____

2. Clarification _____

3. Emphasis _____

Writing with Colons

INSTRUCTIONS:
Use independent clauses with colons to introduce lists of the indicated items. Circle the colons, and don't forget to use your commas correctly.

EXAMPLE: (fruits) I usually eat many different kinds of fruit: strawberries, figs, dates, and apples.

1. (pets) _____

2. (countries) _____

3. (languages) _____

4. (desserts) _____

5. (hobbies) _____

INSTRUCTIONS:
Use colons after independent clauses to add an explanation or emphasis. Circle the colons when you use them. For sentences 4-6, write your own.

EXAMPLE: It was clear what Kevin and his friends wanted to do: play video games and eat chicken tenders.

1. All my life, I've only had one dream. _____

2. Julie gave her mother a very clear request. _____

3. After we really thought about it, the answer was obvious. _____

4. _____

5. _____

6. _____

Grammaropolis

The Big Semicolon and Colon Quiz!

INSTRUCTIONS: Indicate which of the following sentences uses correct **semicolon** punctuation.

1. A. You know martial arts; I need your help with a bully.
   B. You know martial arts, so; I need your help with a bully.
   C. You know martial arts; and I need your help with a bully.

2. A. It snowed all night. As a result; the ground is white.
   B. It snowed all night; as a result, the ground is white.
   C. It snowed all night, as a result; the ground is white.

3. A. Bees pollinate our flowers; and they are essential to the world's ecosystem.
   B. Bees pollinate our flowers; and, they are essential to the world's ecosystem.
   C. Bees pollinate our flowers; they are essential to the world's ecosystem.

4. A. Jaylen read all night; meanwhile, his sister did nothing but watch television.
   B. Jaylen read all night, meanwhile; his sister did nothing but watch television.
   C. Jaylen read all night, meanwhile, his sister did nothing but watch television.

5. A. I don't know how to cook; but, nevertheless, Ian is still my friend.
   B. I don't know how to cook, nevertheless Ian is still my friend.
   C. I don't know how to cook; nevertheless, Ian is still my friend.

INSTRUCTIONS: Indicate which of the following sentences uses correct colon punctuation.

6. A. I many hobbies: knitting, running, and cooking.
   B. I have many hobbies, including: knitting, running, and cooking.
   C. My many hobbies include: knitting, running, and cooking.

7. A. Jason knew what he was looking: for cheese.
   B. Jason knew what he was looking for: cheese.
   C. Jason knew: that he was looking for cheese.

8. A. Candice told me her secret: "I'm exhausted."
   B. Candice told me: her secret, "I'm exhausted."
   C. Candice told me her secret: "I'm exhausted".

9. A. I bought a few groceries: such as ham, cheese, and milk.
   B. I bought a few groceries: ham, cheese, and milk.
   C. I bought a few groceries: such as ham, cheese, and milk.

10. A. There's one thing I know a lot about: it's pudding.
    B. If there's one thing I know a lot about: it's pudding.
    C. There's one thing I know a lot about: pudding.

Meet Police Dog Hyphen

I am a hyphen.

I connect two or more words into a single concept.

I help avoid confusion about what your words mean.

EXAMPLES

WITH ADJECTIVES: My money-saving ideas are strong.

WITH LAST NAMES: Mrs. Jones-Castillo is very friendly.

WITH NUMBERS: I have seventy-three friends.

WITH LETTER COLLISIONS: Do you have any anti-itch cream?

WITH INTERRUPTIONS IN PRINTED TEXT: People think that I don't have spec-tacular ideas often, but I have one now!

Using Hyphens

Use me to connect two or more words into a single concept.

Adjectives:
Jin has a money-making business.

Last Names:
I just met Mrs. Wight-Lopez.

Numbers:
I have twenty-two cats.

Pro Tip:
Hyphens can also be used for extra clarity to highlight letter collisions (re-elect) or to differentiate between homonyms (recover vs. re-cover).

Let's practice!

Instructions:
In each of the following sentences, circle the words that are missing hyphens and then write the correct single concept on the line provided.

EXAMPLE:
Someone gave Taylor (fifty three) roses on his birthday.   fifty-three

1.   Have you ever eaten at the new Spanish French restaurant?   _____

2.   The painter made sure the outside facing walls were painted yellow.   _____

3.   I'm not sure that Mr. Schmidt Nowara is in town today.   _____

4.   Did you just give me the jack o lantern face?   _____

5.   On her thirtieth birthday, Susan stayed at a pig friendly hotel.   _____

Your turn!

Instructions:
Write sentences below using hyphens to join multiple words into an adjective, name, or number. Don't forget to circle your hyphens.

1. adjective _____

2. last name _____

3. number _____

Writing with Hyphens

INSTRUCTIONS:
Circle five of the following hyphenated words and incorporate them into your own sentences. Be sure to circle the hyphens when you use them!

one-sided deep-fried right-handed stomach-churning baby-faced twenty-two seventy-four Spanish-Italian anti-itch panic-inducing great-grandfather light-headed well-worn x-ray

1. _____

2. _____

3. _____

4. _____

5. _____

INSTRUCTIONS:
Write a short story that incorporates at least one hyphenated word in every sentence. You may use any of the words in the box above, but definitely come up with new hyphenated words on your own. Circle all of the hyphens.

_____

_____

_____

_____

_____

_____

_____

Meet Police Dog Dash

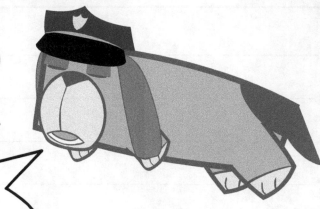

I am a dash.

My bark is louder than a hyphen—you can't miss it.

I can create emphasis, indicate an interruption, or replace other punctuation.

EXAMPLES

CREATING EMPHASIS: I wanted to see a bald eagle on my school trip—I saw six of them!

INDICATING AN INTERRUPTION: "That raccoon will never open my—"

REPLACING PARENTHESES: My grandmother—my mother's mother—is a fantastic tennis player.

REPLACING A COLON: There's only one way for us to break out of this room—magic.

Using Dashes

Use me instead of other punctuation marks when you want to emphasize or call attention to something.

Parentheses:
Our predicament (no water, little food) is precarious at the moment.

Dashes:
Our predicament—no water, little food—is precarious at the moment.

Colon:
I demand one thing: honesty.

Dash:
I demand one thing—honesty.

Pro Tip:
A dash can also indicate an interruption in quoted speech: "Did you know that a dash can indicate—"

Let's practice!

Instructions:
Add dashes to the following sentences where necessary, then circle the dashes.

EXAMPLE:
Jill's restaurant—the most expensive one in the city—is hard to get into.

1. Jacob and his mother who flew all the way from Chicago saw the play last night.

2. Because I had studied so much, the answer came immediately popcorn.

3. I have a car a brand new one, if you can believe it that fits five people.

4. Tree people the kind you find in fantasy novels are generally friendly.

5. He stared at me intently, and I suddenly saw what he saw a tired old man.

Your turn!

Instructions:
Write sentences using dashes for extra emphasis as substitutions for the punctuation marks as indicated. Don't forget to circle the dashes.

1. parentheses _____

2. colon _____

3. parentheses _____

Writing with Dashes

INSTRUCTIONS (PART ONE):
Use a dash instead of a colon to create extra emphasis. Circle the dashes.

EXAMPLE: I knew there could only be one explanation for what I saw—aliens.

1. _____

2. _____

INSTRUCTIONS (PART TWO):
Use a dash instead of parentheses to create extra emphasis. Circle the dashes.

EXAMPLE: My sister's dog—an enormous Rottweiler-Poodle mix—ate my homework.

1. _____

2. _____

INSTRUCTIONS (PART THREE):
Write a short story that incorporates at least three uses of the dash to create emphasis—in place of either parentheses or a colon—and circle all of the dashes.

_____

_____

_____

_____

_____

_____

_____

Grammaropolis

The Big Hyphen and Dash Quiz!

INSTRUCTIONS: Indicate which of the following sentences uses correct **hyphen** punctuation.

1. A. Present-day humans live in the present day.
   B. Present day humans live in the present-day.
   C. Present-day-humans live in the present day.

2. A. Wash your hands, and be careful of flesh-eating-bacteria.
   B. Wash your hands, and be careful of flesh-eating bacteria.
   C. Wash your hands, and be careful of flesh eating bacteria.

3. A. Xavier is a well known singer who is very well-known around the world.
   B. Xavier is a well-known singer who is very well-known around the world.
   C. Xavier is a well-known singer who is very well known around the world.

4. A. My next-door neighbor lives next door to me.
   B. My next door neighbor lives next-door to me.
   C. My next-door neighbor lives next-door to me.

5. A. That "twenty-five-minute" talk went on for thirty five minutes.
   B. That "twenty-five minute" talk went on for thirty five minutes.
   C. That "twenty-five-minute" talk went on for thirty-five minutes.

INSTRUCTIONS: Indicate which of the following sentences uses correct **dash** punctuation.

6. A. What I've been telling you all day—all month, really, is that I don't like soda.
   B. What I've been telling you all day, all month, really—is that I don't like soda.
   C. What I've been telling you all day—all month, really—is that I don't like soda.

7. A. After twenty-two years of searching, I finally found the answer—mangoes.
   B. After twenty-two years of searching—I finally found the answer—mangoes.
   C. After twenty-two years of searching—I finally found the answer—mangoes.

8. A. I have been here a long time—twenty-two years—and I'm not going anywhere else.
   B. I have been here—a long time, twenty-two years—and I'm not going anywhere else.
   C. I have been here a long time—twenty-two years, and I'm not going anywhere else.

9. A. I brought it all—toothbrush, toothpaste—and—floss.
   B. I brought it all—toothbrush, toothpaste—and floss.
   C. I brought it all—toothbrush, toothpaste, and floss.

10. A. That man—my brother—stole from me!
    B. That man, my brother—stole—from me!
    C. That man—my brother, stole from me!

Meet Prosecutor Apostrophe

I am an apostrophe.

I can show possession or make contractions.

EXAMPLES

SHOWING POSSESSION: Nelson's teachers are nice.

MAKING CONTRACTIONS: I don't believe she would've done that.

Using Apostrophes with Contractions

Name:

Use me with contractions to show where one or more letters has been removed.

*I **do not** want to practice piano.*
*Susan **would have** known the answer.*
***Who is** at the door?*
***He will** be here soon.*

*I **don't** want to practice piano.*
*Susan **would've** known the answer.*
***Who's** at the door?*
***He'll** be here soon.*

Pro Tip:
*The contraction of **it is** = **it's**. There's no apostrophe with **its** when showing possession.*

Let's practice!

Instructions:
In each of the following sentences, circle the words that could use an apostrophe for contraction and then write the correct contraction on the line.

EXAMPLE:
Susannah had not eaten a single piece of candy all week.   _____hadn't_____

1.   I would rather not go there.   _____

2.   Jacob asked Sophie if she thought they would arrive early.   _____

3.   Some people do not like chocolate at all.   _____

4.   Fatinha can not believe how silly the play is.   _____

5.   Most teachers genuinely think they are nice people.   _____

Your turn!

Instructions:
Write the correct contractions for the following words in the spaces provided. Circle the apostrophes!

1. should have _____   4. they are _____   7. should not _____

2. let us _____   5. we will _____   8. did not _____

3. I am _____   6. they had _____   9. will not _____

Using Apostrophes to Show Possession

Name:

Use me to create possessive forms.

Singular Nouns:
the **dog's** bark
James's toys

Plural Nouns:
the **teachers'** rules
the **birds'** migration

Shared Possession:
Will and Ed's adventure
(one adventure shared by both)
Will's and Ed's adventures
(Will's adventure and
Ed's adventure)

Pro Tip:
There's no apostrophe with *its* when showing possession. *It's* is a contraction.

Let's practice!

Instructions: Add and circle any missing apostrophes where they're needed to show possession.

EXAMPLE:
I want to play with Julian's new toy car.

1. How nice of you to fill the cats bowl! *(one cat)*

2. The kids are so happy! They feel like they're soaring on eagles wings. *(multiple eagles)*

3. Ians room is bigger than his sister Paulas room.

4. I love spending time at Ian and Paulas house.

5. The dog wagged its tail when it smelled Sandras moms cooking.

Your turn!

Instructions: Use apostrophes to show possession for the following items.

1. Bob/turtle _____Bob's turtle_____

2. Jay and Ed/cats (separate) _____

3. Ellis/hat _____

4. goose/beak _____

5. dog and cat/owner (shared) _____

6. jack-in-the-box/spring _____

Writing with Apostrophes

INSTRUCTIONS (PART ONE):

Write five sentences using apostrophes to make contractions. Be sure to circle all of the apostrophes.

1. _____

2. _____

3. _____

4. _____

5. _____

INSTRUCTIONS (PART TWO):

Write five sentences using apostrophes to show possession of the following items. Be sure to circle all of the apostrophes.

1. sandwich _____

2. toes _____

3. homework _____

4. parents _____

5. ideas _____

INSTRUCTIONS (PART THREE):

Write a sentence that includes at least two apostrophes making a contraction and at least two apostrophes indicating possession. Circle the contractions and underline the words showing possession.

_____

_____

_____

_____

The Big Apostrophe Quiz!

INSTRUCTIONS: *Indicate which of the following sentences uses correct apostrophe punctuation.*

1. A. Samuel's sister doesnt talk very much about sporting events.
    B. Samuels' sister doesn't talk very much about sporting events.
    C. Samuel's sister doesn't talk very much about sporting events.

2. A. I love Jason's house, but I don't really like Sis's house.
    B. I love Jason's house, but I don't really like Sis' house.
    C. I love Jason's house, but I dont really like Sis's house.

3. A. Its really stressful whenever Kyle's phone's battery loses its charge.
    B. It's really stressful whenever Kyle's phone's battery loses it's charge.
    C. It's really stressful whenever Kyle's phone's battery loses its charge.

4. A. There is only one book, and it's Stephen's and Jess's book.
    B. There is only one book, and it's Stephen and Jess' book.
    C. There is only one book, and it's Stephen and Jess's book.

5. A. I'm a big fan of both Carlos's and Zeke's two different ideas .
    B. I'm a big fan of both Carlos and Zeke's two different ideas.
    C. Im a big fan of both Carlos's and Zeke's two different ideas.

6. A. Haven't we heard enough from the children's classroom already?
    B. Havent we heard enough from the children's classroom already?
    C. Haven't we heard enough from the childrens' classroom already?

7. A. He's serious about wanting to read all of Mrs. Gomez' books.
    B. Hes serious about wanting to read all of Mrs. Gomez's books.
    C. He's serious about wanting to read all of Mrs. Gomez's books.

8. A. Let's agree to disagree; I'm sure there's no reason to fight.
    B. Lets agree to disagree; I'm sure there's no reason to fight.
    C. Let's agree to disagree; I'm sure theres no reason to fight.

9. A. It's amazing how fast a hummingbird flaps it's wings.
    B. Its amazing how fast a hummingbird flaps it's wings.
    C. It's amazing hoe fast a hummingbird flaps its wings.

10. A. Don't look now, but Lisas coming here with Bob's spatula.
    B. Don't look now, but Lisa's coming here with Bob's spatula.
    C. Don't look now, but Lisa's coming here with Bobs spatula.

Meet Court Reporter Quotation Marks

I am a quotation mark.

I always come in pairs.

I can set apart a direct quotation or indicate technical terms and words used in an unusual way.

EXAMPLES

SETTING APART A DIRECT QUOTATION: My sister said, "I don't feel like sharing my taffy with you."

INDICATING A TECHNICAL TERM: "Cryptozoology" is the study of creatures from folklore.

INDICATING A NICKNAME: I love rooting for Ed "Too Tall" Jones.

INDICATING SARCASM: Yeah, it's really "smart" to steal things.

Using Quotation Marks with Direct Quotations

Use me to set apart a direct quotation.

"Do you know who I am?" Julie asked.
Bob responded, "I don't think so."

Punctuation Outside:
Introductory Commas and Colons
I said, "Don't do that."
Julie commanded: "Stop!"

Punctuation Inside:
Commas, Exclamation Marks, and Question Marks
"Don't do that," I said.
"Stop!" Julie commanded.

Pro Tip:
Use single quotation marks when putting a quotation within a quotation.

Let's practice!

Instructions:
Add quotation marks to the following sentences if they are needed, then circle all of the quotation marks that you've added.

EXAMPLE:
"Nope," Zakir said. "I don't think we're going home right now."

1. Julian yelled across the room, No way!

2. Hooray! Alvin said. I'm free.

3. Have you ever been to Colorado? Abel asked.

4. Don't bother me Irene said while waving the kids away.

5. I wish you could spend the night. I want to have a pillow fight, Blake said.

Your turn!

Instructions:
Write three sentences using quotation marks to set apart a direct quotation. Remember to punctuate correctly and circle the quotation marks.

1. _____

2. _____

3. _____

Other Uses for Quotation Marks

Use me with technical terms, nicknames, or language used in an unusual way.

Technical Terms:
Scientists discovered "studiavirus," a new virus that helps people learn.

Nicknames:
My dad was known as Gregory "Two Shoes" McMahon.

Sarcasm:
We "studied" at Sandra's birthday party.

Pro Tip:
Quotation marks used to add emphasis are sometimes called "scare quotes."

Let's practice!

Instructions:
Add quotation marks to the following sentences if they are needed, then circle all of the quotation marks that you've added.

EXAMPLE:

Scotty's childhood friends always referred to him as "Pale Fox."

1. The boy practiced defenestration, the act of throwing something out of a window.

2. My name is Rick, but you can call me Silly Pants.

3. Oh yeah, the kids sure are responsible when they play with fire like that.

4. Please meet my friend Jackie The Spy Patterson.

5. Looking one time at the packing list isn't really what I'd call preparing.

Your turn!

Instructions:
Write three sentences using quotation marks as described above. Don't forget to circle the quotation marks!

1. _____

2. _____

3. _____

Grammaropolis

Writing with Quotation Marks

Name:

INSTRUCTIONS:

Use quotation marks to properly punctuate the following dialogue as sentences in a story. You may add any creative elements you wish: action, character and setting description, or dialogue tags (said, shouted, asked).

ZOLA: Can you give me a hand with this box?

HANK: What's in it?

ZOLA: I don't know, but it's heavy.

HANK: Don't you want to see what's inside?

ZOLA: The last time someone opened one of these boxes, a lion jumped out.

HANK: Lions are cute. Please?

ZOLA: Okay. What could go wrong?

_____

_____

_____

_____

_____

_____

_____

_____

_____

Grammaropolis

The Big Quotation Marks Quiz!

INSTRUCTIONS: Indicate which of the following sentences punctuates quotation marks correctly.

1. A. Sylvia said, "I don't think there's anything to worry about."
    B. Sylvia said she "doesn't think there's anything" to worry about.
    C. Sylvia said, "I don't think there's anything to worry about.

2. A. "I don't think you're right" I said sadly.
    B. "I don't think you're right," I said sadly.
    C. 'I don't think you're right,' I said sadly.

3. A. "Of course"! Julie exclaimed. "There's hidden treasure under the 'X'!"
    B. "Of course!" Julie exclaimed. "There's hidden treasure under the 'X'!"
    C. "Of course!" Julie exclaimed. "There's hidden treasure under the "X"!"

4. A. "Do you have something to say to me?" Alvin asked with a smile.
    B. "Do you have something to say to me"? Alvin asked with a smile.
    C. "Do you have something to say to me," Alvin asked with a smile?

5. A. Jake said, "Alvin asked me, 'Do you have anything to say to me?'"
    B. Jake said, "Alvin asked me, 'Do you have anything to say to me'?"
    C. Jake said, "Alvin asked me, "Do you have anything to say to me?""

6. A. "Someone needs to come home", my mom said, "and that someone is you!"
    B. "Someone needs to come home," my mom said, "and that someone is you!"
    C. "Someone needs to come home," my mom said, "and that someone is you"!

7. A. "Have some cheese," Vinny yelled at us!
    B. "Have some cheese"! Vinny yelled at us.
    C. "Have some cheese!" Vinny yelled at us.

8. A. "Watching television is not 'studying' at all!" my mom said.
    B. "Watching television is not "studying" at all!" my mom said.
    C. 'Watching television is not "studying" at all!' my mom said.

9. A. "Hey, you!" I yelled. "Put the book down!"
    B. "Hey, you," I yelled! "Put the book down!"
    C. "Hey, you!" I yelled. "Put the book down"!

10. A. Lyall gave me her final answer: "It's not a salamander."
    B. Lyall gave me her final answer: "It's not a salamander".
    C. Lyall gave me her final answer,: "it's not a salamander."

We are parentheses.

We enclose nonessential information.

We can indicate a clarification or an aside or afterthought.

PUBLIC DEFENSE
PARENTHESES BRACKETS

EXAMPLES

INDICATING A CLARIFICATION: Sally (my sister) bought that mug from her favorite store (the one around the corner).

INDICATING AN ASIDE OR AFTERTHOUGHT: The decision Julian made (a decision that everyone knew was going to be a disaster, by the way) was what got him into so much trouble.

Using Parentheses with Nonessential Information

Use us to set apart nonessential information, such as a clarification or an aside or afterthought.

Clarification:
José (my brother) bought us all chocolate muffins.

Aside or Afterthought:
They studied (more like watched TV, really) at Janice's house for the big quiz.

Pro Tip:
If the words inside the parentheses don't make a complete sentence, the end marks come outside.

Let's practice!

Instructions:
Add parentheses to enclose any nonessential information in the following sentences, then circle all of the parentheses that you've added.

EXAMPLE:
My sister (the one with brown hair) was laughing all night.

1. There is nobody I trust more than Jake my little brother.

2. James always eats breakfast he loves pancakes even if he's not hungry.

3. Nobody but Amy the founder of the fan club can admit new members.

4. Yishan went home early yesterday really early to water her plants.

5. Chocolate cakes especially the ones with sprinkles make people happy.

Your turn!

Instructions:
Write sentences that incorporate the nonessential information enclosed in the parentheses below.

1. (not that I believed him) _____

2. (Tuesday morning) _____

3. (in France) _____

The Punctuation Workbook, Grades 3-5 © 2020 by Grammaropolis 49

Writing with Parentheses

Name:

INSTRUCTIONS (PART ONE):
Write four sentences that don't contain parentheses.

EXAMPLE: _____ Kelvin spoke to my history teacher after school today. _____

1. _____

2. _____

3. _____

4. _____

INSTRUCTIONS (PART TWO):
Now add parentheses to each of your sentences above to enclose nonessential information, such as a clarification or an aside or afterthought. Circle the parentheses.

EXAMPLE: _____ Kelvin spoke to my history teacher (the guy who always gives me way worse grades than I

deserve) after school today. _____

1. _____

_____

2. _____

_____

3. _____

_____

4. _____

Grammaropolis

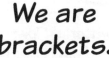

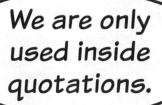

We are brackets.

We are only used inside quotations.

We can be used to clarify, indicate a grammar mistake, or make quoted material flow with the rest of the text.

EXAMPLES

CLARIFYING: Janice said, "I don't think they [her cousins] are coming to the reunion."

INDICATING A GRAMMAR MISTAKE: "Some snakes shed they're [sic] skin every couple of months."

MAKING QUOTED MATERIAL FLOW: Steven told me yesterday that, "[s]ome parrots have enormous vocabularies."

Using Brackets

Use us inside quotation marks to enclose a clarification, make quoted material flow, or to indicate a grammar mistake.

Clarification:
"They went there [Bob's attic] to find old toys,"

Quoted Material Flow:
Jason said, "[his] dad is hilarious."

Grammar Mistake:
"Bob goed [sic] to his house for dinner."

Pro Tip:
Brackets are only used inside quotation marks.

Let's practice!

Instructions:
Add brackets to the following sentences where appropriate, then circle all of the brackets that you've added.

EXAMPLE:
Jaylen pleaded, "Don't give her [Patricia] a single marshmallow!"

1. "Theodore runned sic away," cried the little boy.

2. Peter shouted, "Get out of here Peter's room."

3. Janice told me last night, "Don't worry, she Janice's mom knows how to cook."

4. "Spencer promise sic to give me a big raise."

5. "I've never been here the post office on a Tuesday."

Your turn!

Instructions:
Write sentences that incorporate the information in the brackets below. Don't forget to use quotation marks!

1. [sic] _____

2. [Peter's dog] _____

3. [a small sculpture found in Italy] _____

Grammaropolis

Writing with Brackets

INSTRUCTIONS:
Use brackets to add information to the following quotations. Indicate grammar mistakes wherever necessary and add any clarifying information wherever you feel is appropriate. Don't forget to circle the brackets you use.

1. "Of course," Katrina said. "Suki took me there for my twelfth birthday."

_____

_____

2. My friend complains a lot about living in Houston: "The worst thing about this place are the heat."

_____

_____

3. "The disaster that struck our town last year was devastating."

_____

_____

4. "Most scientists agreed that the results of their experiment were not surprising."

_____

_____

5. "That teacher made me put it back in my backpack until the end of class."

_____

_____

Grammaropolis

The Big Parentheses and Brackets Quiz!

INSTRUCTIONS: Indicate which of the following sentences uses correct parentheses punctuation.

1. A. Most computers (if they are not too old) will run this program.
   B. Most computers (If they are not too old) will run this program.
   C. Most computers (if they are not too old,) will run this program.

2. A. He was really, really old (13. To be exact.)
   B. He was really, really old (13, to be exact.)
   C. He was really, really old (13, to be exact).

3. A. He still hadn't graded our papers. (He was over a month late!)
   B. He still hadn't graded our papers (he was over a month late)!
   C. He still hadn't graded our papers. (He was over a month late)!

4. A. Most people (including Morgan) don't like jalapeño sprinkles on their cupcakes.
   B. Most people including (Morgan) don't like jalapeño sprinkles on their cupcakes.
   C. Most people (including) Morgan, don't like jalapeño sprinkles on their cupcakes.

5. A. Elvira gave Samuel a t-shirt in his favorite color (blue).
   B. Elvira gave Samuel a t-shirt in his favorite color (Blue!)
   C. Elvira gave Samuel a t-shirt in his favorite color (blue.)

INSTRUCTIONS: Indicate which of the following sentences uses correct brackets punctuation.

6. A. That's not his [Jason's] toy train.
   B. "That's not his toy train [Jason's]."
   C. "That's not his [Jason's] toy train."

7. A. "The whole class went to they're house for dinner."
   B. "The whole class went to they're [their] house for dinner."
   C. "The whole class went to they're [sic] house for dinner."

8. A. I saw a note on the door: "Dont [sic] come in here."
   B. I saw a note on the door: "Dont [Don't] come in here."
   C. I saw a note on the door: "Dont [misspelling of don't] come in here

9. A. Janet said, "Please take her [Janet's sister] the assignment."
   B. Janet said, "Please take her [my sister] the assignment."
   C. Janet asked us to take her [Janet's sister] the assignment.

10. A. Billy yelled, "Someone come here!" [Billy's hotel room]
    B. Billy yelled, "Someone come here [Billy's hotel room]!"
    C. Billy yelled, "Someone come here [Billy's hotel room!]"

Grammaropolis

Capitalization

Capitalization is important.

Capital letters can indicate the beginning of a sentence, a proper noun, or a proper adjective.

EXAMPLES

BEGINNING OF A SENTENCE: Most cars have four wheels.

PROPER NOUN: I offered Nelson a sip of my Sprite.

PROPER ADJECTIVE: The Spanish class is empty today.

Using Proper Capitalization

We always capitalize proper nouns, proper adjectives, and the first letter of every sentence.

Sentences:
Please help me with this.
Do you want some guava juice?

Proper Nouns:
Paulo is from Italy.
He studies the Renaissance.

Proper Adjectives:
Paulo is Italian.
He loves Renaissance paintings.

Pro Tip:
A proper adjective is the adjective form of a proper noun or a proper noun used as an adjective.

Let's practice!

Instructions:
Double underline and circle any capitalization mistakes in the following sentences.

EXAMPLE:
some people don't like russian food, but I love it.

1. do you enjoy eating new mexican food when you visit your cousin in albuquerque?

2. the other day, i went to see dr. smith over on delaware st.

3. we learned a lot about the spanish-american war.

4. I think it's important for everyone to read monster by walter dean myers.

5. my favorite band is the smashing pumpkins. Are they irish?

Your turn!

Instructions:
Write three sentences that incorporate proper nouns, proper adjectives, or both. Circle every capitalized letter you use.

1. _____

2. _____

3. _____

Capitalization in Writing

INSTRUCTIONS (PART ONE):

Brainstorm a collection of proper nouns and proper adjectives. Remember that proper nouns and proper adjectives are capitalized. Once you've finished, circle three words from each collection.

PROPER NOUNS

Argentina

PROPER ADJECTIVES

Shakespearean

INSTRUCTIONS (PART TWO):

Write a short story that incorporates all of the words you have circled above. When you have finished writing your story, circle all of the capital letters. Don't forget the capital words to start each sentence, along with all the proper nouns and proper adjectives.

The Big Capitalization Quiz!

INSTRUCTIONS: Indicate which of the following sentences uses correct capitalization.

1. A. my sister gave me a sparkling pony for Christmas.
   B. All I wanted for christmas was a sparkling pony.
   C. The best thing about Christmas was the sparkling pony my sister gave me.

2. A. Let's eat italian food.
   B. Of course! i love Italian food!.
   C. What is your favorite kind of Italian food?

3. A. Do you know how to sing the national anthem of Mexico?
   B. I have never sung the mexican national anthem.
   C. the Mexican national anthem is beautiful.

4. A. my favorite part of the movie was when the main character went to Arizona.
   B. In most movies, people don't go to Arizona.
   C. Did you know that people from Arizona are called arizonians?

5. A. Arush flew all the way to Oregon to sing in the choir.
   B. I wonder why arush had to go to Oregon to sing.
   C. The best part about Arush singing in oregon is that he got to visit Portland.

6. A. I speak spanish, italian, and japanese.
   B. I speak Spanish, Italian, and Japanese.
   C. i speak Spanish, Italian, and Japanese.

7. A. Our class is taking a trip to Albuquerque, new Mexico.
   B. I can't wait for our class trip to Albuquerque, New mexico.
   C. I have heard so much about the wonderful food in Albuquerque, New Mexico.

8. A. why are you looking at me like that?
   B. It feels like you are giving Me the evil eye.
   C. Please stop looking at me like that.

9. A. Kevin had never been to a renaissance fair before.
   B. He had heard about Renaissance fairs, but had never been to one.
   C. I told kevin that he should definitely go.

10. A. Please spend time studying for your Latin test.
    B. Some people say that latin is a dead language.
    C. I would never say that, but if I did, mr. White would be sad.

Abbreviation

Abbreviations are the shortened forms of words or phrases.

Most of the time, you'll use a period to indicate abbreviation.

EXAMPLES

PERSONAL NAMES: John C. Reilly, E. Lockhart

TITLES: Dr. Jacobsen, Mrs. McKenzie

ADDRESSES: 224 Grammar St.

ORGANIZATIONS: Good Times, Inc.

Using Abbreviation

We can use abbreviations to save space and avoid repetition.

Titles:
Doctor -> Dr.
Esquire -> Esq.

Initials:
Susan Eloise Hinton -> S.E. Hinton
Alan Alexander Milne -> A.A. Milne

Addresses:
Banks Street -> Banks St.
Baltic Avenue -> Baltic Ave.

Pro Tip:
Most of the time, you'll use a period to indicate an abbreviation.

Let's practice!

Instructions:
Circle any word that could be abbreviated and write the correct abbreviation in the space provided.

EXAMPLE:
Send me to (Doctor) Bronstein's office.   _____Dr._____

1.   Do you have Mister Reynolds for English class?   _____

2.   My name is Evelyn Rose Rodgers.   _____

3.   I went to Missus Jin's house on Franklin Street.   _____

4.   Can you please put me in touch with Reverend Smithers?   _____

5.   I learned a lot about Saint Thomas from reading this book.   _____

Your turn!

Instructions:
Write the correct abbreviations for the following words in the spaces provided.

1. Road _____   4. Doctor _____   7. Drive _____

2. Avenue _____   5. Junior _____   8. Court _____

3. Mister _____   6. Senior _____   9. Missus _____

Abbreviation in Writing

INSTRUCTIONS (PART ONE):
Brainstorm a collection of abbreviations in the categories below. Once you've finished, circle two abbreviations from each column.

TITLES	ADDRESSES	NAMES w/ INITIALS	COMPANIES
Mrs.	Ave.	D.B. Sweeny	Corp.

INSTRUCTIONS (PART TWO):
Write a short story that incorporates all of the words you have circled above. When you have finished writing your story, circle all of the abbreviations you've used.

_____

_____

_____

_____

_____

_____

_____

_____

_____

Grammaropolis

The Big Abbreviation Quiz!

INSTRUCTIONS: Indicate which of the following sentences uses correct abbreviation punctuation.

1. A. Have you ever been to Mister Johnson's shoe store?
   B. Have you ever been to Mr. Johnson's shoe store?
   C. Have you ever been to Mist. Johnson's shoe store?

2. A. Jake lives on Castle Ct.
   B. Jake lives on Castle Crt.
   C. Jake lives on Castle Court.

3. A. Please send this directly to Campbell Cupcake Cmpny.
   B. Please send this directly to Campbell Cupcake Co.
   C. Please send this directly to Campbell Cupcake Cy.

4. A. I have addressed my letter to Bill S. Preston, Esq.
   B. I have addressed my letter to Bill S Preston, Esq.
   C. I have addressed my letter to Bill S. Preston, Esqre.

5. A. My favorite writer is definitely JK Rowling.
   B. My favorite writer is definitely JK. Rowling.
   C. My favorite writer is definitely J.K. Rowling

INSTRUCTIONS: Choose the correct answers to the questions below.

6. What is the correct abbreviation for Doctor?
   A. Dr.   C. dr.
   B. Dctr.   D. Dr

7. What is the correct abbreviation for boulevard?
   A. blvd.   C. Boul.
   B. Blvd.   D. Bl.

8. What is the correct abbreviation for Missus?
   A. Miss   C. Mrs.
   B. Mrs   D. Mis.

9. What is the correct abbreviation for Incorporated?
   A. inc   C. Inc.
   B. Incorp.   D. Inc

10. What is the correct abbreviation for Mister?
    A. Mist.   C. mr.
    B. M.   D. Mr.

Grammaropolis

The Big Quiz Answer Key!

END MARKS

1. B	6. A
2. A	7. C
3. B	8. A
4. A	9. C
5. C	

COMMAS

1. B	6. B
2. A	7. A
3. B	8. C
4. A	9. A
5. A	10. A

SEMICOLONS & COLONS

1. A	6. A
2. B	7. B
3. C	8. A
4. A	9. B
5. C	10. C

HYPHENS & DASHES

1. A	6. C
2. B	7. A
3. C	8. A
4. A	9. C
5. C	10. A

APOSTROPHES

1. C	5. A	9. C
2. A	6. A	10. B
3. C	7. C	
4. C	8. A	

QUOTATION MARKS

1. A	5. A	9. A
2. B	6. B	10. A
3. B	7. C	
4. A	8. A	

PARENTHESES & BRACKETS

1. A	5. A	9. A
2. C	6. C	10. B
3. A	7. C	
4. A	8. A	

CAPITALIZATION

1. C	5. A	9. B
2. C	6. B	10. A
3. A	7. C	
4. B	8. C	

ABBREVIATION

1. B	5. C	9. C
2. A	6. A	10. D
3. B	7. B	
4. A	8. C	

GRAMMAR CURRICULUM CHECKLIST

- ☑ Innovative and engaging
- ☑ Aligned to state standards
- ☑ Addresses various learning styles
- ☑ Created and refined in the ultimate proving grounds: the classroom

THE STORYBOOKS

4/24/2019 | $6.99
Paperback | 32 pages | 8" x 8"
Full-color illustrations throughout
Includes instructional back matter
Ages 7 to 11 | Grades 1 to 5
JUVENILE NONFICTION /
LANGUAGE ARTS / GRAMMAR

9781644420157 | Noun
9781644420171 | Verb
9781644420133 | Adjective
9781644420102 | Adverb
9781644420164 | Pronoun
9781644420119 | Conjunction
9781644420140 | Preposition
9781644420126 | Interjection

- An eight-book series starring the parts of speech, which are personified based on the roles they play in the sentence.

- Featuring a different character-based adventure for every part of speech.

- Each book includes standards–aligned definitions and examples, just like you'd find in a textbook (but way more fun).

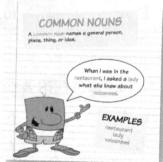

THE WORKBOOKS

3/03/2020 | $12.99 | B&W
PB | 64 pages | 11"H x 8.5"W
Includes quizzes & instruction
Ages 7 to 11 | Grades 1 to 5
JUVENILE NONFICTION /
LANGUAGE ARTS / GRAMMAR

9781644420300 | Grade 1
9781644420317 | Grade 2
9781644420324 | Grade 3
9781644420331 | Grade 4
9781644420188 | Grade 5

- Skill-building workbooks featuring character-based instruction along with various comprehension checks and writing exercises.

- Aligned to Common Core and state standards for K–5.

Grammaropolis is available through Ingram Publisher Services.
Contact your IPS Sales Representative to order.
Call (866) 400-5351, Fax (800) 838-1149, ips@ingramcontent.com, or visit ipage.

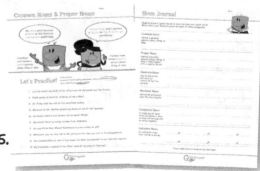

Printed in the USA
CPSIA information can be obtained
at www.ICGtesting.com
JSHW060239160824
68134JS00058BA/2680